YOUR KNOWLEDGE HAS VALUE

The American Dream in the Speech "Yes we can" by Barack Obama

A short analysis

Luisa Grötsch

Bibliographic information published by the German National Library:

The German National Library lists this publication in the National Bibliography; detailed bibliographic data are available on the Internet at http://dnb.dnb.de.

ISBN: 9783346276902
This book is also available as an ebook.

© GRIN Publishing GmbH
Nymphenburger Straße 86
80636 München

Print and binding: Books on Demand GmbH, Norderstedt, Germany
Printed on acid-free paper from responsible sources.

The present work has been carefully prepared. Nevertheless, authors and publishers do not incur liability for the correctness of information, notes, links and advice as well as any printing errors.

GRIN web shop: https://www.grin.com/document/937090

The influence of the "American Dream" on Barack Obama's "Yes, we can" speech

Table of Contents

1   Introduction

The 2008 presidential election in the United States of America was dominated for a long time by the primaries[1] of the Democratic Party with a fierce competition between a white woman, Hillary Clinton, and the African American senator Barack Obama. The extraordinary situation that neither an African American male nor a Caucasian woman had ever been nominated for presidential candidate by the same major political party, caused a great stir, both nationally and internationally.[2]

The New Hampshire primary has traditionally been the first in a series of nation-wide state primary elections. The primary process is used to select the presidential candidates for both Democrats and Republicans depending upon the percentage of state-wide votes that a candidate receives. As the first in a series of primary elections, the New Hampshire primary is viewed as a critical one. The winner obtains a large advantage in the course of the ongoing campaign, because it reflects the opinion of the voters about the candidates for the first time. That is why the New Hampshire primary has such a high level of media attention.[3] On 8 January 2008 Hillary Clinton managed to beat the favored Barack Obama in the New Hampshire primary election. The same day Barack Obama gave his truly inspirational "Yes, we can" speech to his supporters.[4]

This speech is the main topic of my research paper. The two introductory chapters will give a short overview on Barack Obama's life, and then the basics of the "American Dream" will be described.

In the main part, there are two central questions I want to analyse. Firstly, how Barack Obama used the concept of the "American Dream" in order to deliver the key messages in his "Yes, we can" speech. The second question involves a statement that Hillary Clinton made during the primary campaign for the Democratic presidential nomination. As his opponent, she claimed that Barack Obama was "all rhetoric, no substance"[5]. I will explore if these accusations were correct by analysing how Barack Obama fulfilled the promises he made in his New Hampshire speech during his presidency in terms of the "American Dream".

---

[1] Candidates for U.S. President seek their party's nomination in primary elections. See Britannica Encyclopedia, *Primary election*, p. 1.
[2] See Frank, H. (2008) *Rhetorische Analyse der "Yes we can" Rede von Barack Obama.* Norderstedt: Grin Verlag, p. 1.
[3] See Murse, T. (2018) *Why the New Hampshire Primary is so Important*, p. 1ff.
[4] See Frank, H. (2008) p. 4.
[5] Hayes, S. F. (2008) *Obama and the Power of Words*, p. 2.

There is extensive literature both on Barack Obama's life and the "American Dream". For my analysis and understanding of his ideas on the "American Dream" I concentrate on Barack Obama's own biography *Dreams from My Father*, his book *Audacity of Hope* describing his thoughts of reclaiming the "American Dream", and Jim Cullen's often cited book *The American Dream*. The main sources for the analysis of the speech are Harald Frank's book *Rhetorische Analyse der "Yes we can" Rede von Barack Obama* and Shel Leanne's book *Say it like Obama*. For the concluding evaluation of Barack Obama's political achievements various articles and statistical data are used.

2   Barack Obama's biography

Barack Obama's life and personality are characterized by a broadly diverse set of experiences that shaped his view on the "American Dream".

Barack Obama comes from a mixed family. His father, the Kenyan Barack Obama Sr., met his white U.S. born mother Ann Dunham at the University of Hawaii.[6] In 1961, Barack Obama was born in Honolulu, Hawaii. Early in his childhood, after his parents divorced, Barack Obama lived with his mother and his Indonesian Muslim stepfather in Indonesia.[7] Later, due to the fact that his mother wanted Barack Obama to attend an American school, he stayed with his maternal grandparents in the United States of America.[8]

Barack Obama had an excellent school and academic education. He studied political science receiving a bachelor's degree from Columbia University, New York. Afterwards he studied, and excelled, at Harvard University's Law School where he was also named president of the prestigious Harvard Law Review.[9]

After his first studies, he worked as a community organizer[10] in Chicago for three years. It was the time when he converted to Christianity and joined the Trinity United Church of Christ.[11] After he received his law degree he worked as a lawyer and lectured constitutional law.[12]

In 1992, he married Michelle Robinson[13] with whom he has two daughters. In 1995, he published his autobiography *Dreams from My Father*, which mainly discusses the self-discovery of his origins; in particular of his African ancestry. In 2006, his second book *The Audacity of Hope*[14] was published describing his ideas about how politics and civic life should change in the United States of America.[15]

Barack Obama started his political career serving in the Illinois State Senate from 1996 to 2004. He was elected to U.S. Senate in 2004, became president of the United States in 2009 and was re-elected in 2012.[16] In 2009, Barack Obama won the Nobel Peace Prize to honour his remarkable work to improve international diplomacy as well as the cooperation between people from around the globe.[17]

---

[6] See Obama, B. (2004) *Dreams from My Father*, p. 9f.
[7] See Wallenfeldt, J., & Mendell, D. (2019) *Barack Obama*, p.4.
[8] See Obama, B. (2004) p. 54f.
[9] See Wallenfeldt, J., & Mendell, D. (2019) p. 4f.
[10] Someone who identifies community concerns and coordinates efforts of local residents to improve the interests of the community. See Black, C (2019) *The Birthplace of Community Organizing*, p. 2f.
[11] See Obama, B. (2008) *The Audacity of Hope*, p. 206ff.
[12] See Wallenfeldt, J., & Mendell, D. (2019) p. 4ff.
[13] See Obama, B. (2004) p. 440f.
[14] See Frank, H. (2008) p. 2.
[15] See Obama, B. (2008) p. 9ff.
[16] See Wallenfeldt, J., & Mendell, D. (2019) p. 1ff.
[17] See Rodrigues, J. (2017) *The Obama years: timeline of a presidency*, p. 2ff.

3 The "American Dream"

The "American Dream" as an idea and a goal has been present for a long time in the mind of the American people but the origin of the term 'American Dream" only dates back to the beginning of the 20th century. The American historian James Truslow Adams popularized the term in his book THE EPIC OF AMERICA, published in 1931.[18] Truslow described which characteristics and values were typical for Americans:

> "[…] in especial, of that American dream of a better, richer, and happier life for all our citizens of every rank which is the greatest contribution we have as yet made to the thought and welfare of the world."[19]

After Truslow's book, the concept of the "American Dream" was further described by numerous authors. One of the most prominent of these was Jim Cullen. According to Cullen, in his book *The American Dream*[20] the dream of the good life in America started with the Pilgrims and Puritans in the early 17th century as a quest for religious freedom. Later freedom became a central demand of minorities such as African Americans.[21]

Cullen also defines the United States Declaration of Independence, adopted on 4 July 1776, as the charter for the "American Dream". The key concepts that guarantee the "American Dream" are written in its preamble:[22]

> "We hold these truths to be self-evident, that all men are created equal, that they are endowed by their Creator with certain unalienable Rights, that among these are Life, Liberty and the pursuit of Happiness."[23]

However, at that time even the Declaration of Independence proclaimed only that all men are created equal, and more specifically solely white males. The result was that females, African Americans or even Native Americans were not considered to be equal.[24]

Next, Cullen discusses "upward mobility", which for many is the most relevant aspect of the "American Dream". It is typically understood to be an economic and/or social advancement.[25]

---

[18] See Wilson, K. D. (2013) *The American Dream: In the age of diminished expectations*, p. 1.
[19] Truslow, A. J. (1931) THE EPIC OF AMERICA, preface viii.
[20] Full title: *The American Dream. A Short History of an Idea That Shaped a Nation* published in 2003.
[21] See Cullen, J. (2004) *The American Dream: A Short History of an Idea That Shaped a Nation*, p. 15ff.
[22] See Cullen, J. (2004) p. 35ff.
[23] National Archives (Ed.). *Declaration of Independence*.
[24] See Cullen, J. (2004) p. 51.
[25] See Cullen, J. (2004) p. 59f.

A further element defining the American identity is "The American's Creed" written by William Page which passed as a resolution by the United States House of Representatives in 1918. It is a creed similar to a religious creed summing up the principles of the American political faith:[26]

> "I believe in the United States of America as a government of the people, by people, for the people [...] established upon those principles of freedom, equality, justice, and humanity for which American Patriots sacrificed their lives and fortunes."[27]

Central to the "American Dream" is the goal of equality. In the chapter "King of America The Dream of Equality" Cullen discusses the situation of African Americans and women.[28] Cullen states that the "American Dream is in many ways a story of omissions"[29] as inequalities of opportunities have been central for American women[30] and that:

> "The struggle for black equality is one of the great dramas of our national history".[31]

One of the most famous American civil rights activists, Martin Luther King Jr., addressed the fight for racial and social equality in his celebrated "I Have a Dream" speech in 1963:[32]

> "I have a dream that one day this nation will rise up and live out the true meaning of its creed: 'We hold these truths to be self-evident, that all men are created equal'."[33]

Finally, one can summarize that today the "American Dream" means different things to different groups of people, but at its core, it is the idea that every person regardless of their gender, race, creed, colour, origin or sexual orientation should have an equal opportunity to achieve their personal highest aspirations and goals.

Taking into account the principles described above, Barack Obama's life is a prime example for the realization of the "American Dream". Despite coming from a minority, he achieved upward mobility in particular because of his excellent education and his passion to believe in change.

---

[26] See Courtright Patton, M. (2010) *The American's Creed*, p. 1ff.
[27] Page, W. (1917) *The American's Creed*, p.1.
[28] See Cullen, J. (2004) p. 103ff.
[29] Cullen, J (2004) p. 119.
[30] See Cullen, J. (2004) p. 119.
[31] Cullen, J. (2004) p. 110.
[32] See Cullen, J. (2004) p. 125f.
[33] King Jr., Martin L. *"American Rhetoric."* 28 August 1963, p. 4.

4 Barack Obama's "Yes we can" speech

This chapter will analyse how Barack Obama used the concept of the "American Dream" in order to deliver the key messages in his "Yes, we can" speech.

4.1 America's situation when the speech was given

The historical situation in which Barack Obama delivered his speech can be divided into two aspects. On the one hand, the overall situation in the United States of America at the time of the 2008 presidential election and, on the other hand, the specific situation of the primaries for the nomination of a presidential candidate for the Democratic Party. Both aspects strongly influenced his speech.[34]

The overall situation for the 2008 presidential election showed a turbulent picture. The World Trade Center terror attack of 11 September 2001 was still on the mind of the people and there was public anxiety over terrorism and public security. American troops were still stationed in Iraq – an engagement that the majority of the Americans meanwhile opposed. Many Americans distrusted the government to solve problems, for instance rising housing prices, health care disparity, weak economic conditions, and a rapidly increasing unemployment rate.[35]

Voters were looking for candidates they trusted in order to make America a safe place. Furthermore, there was an increased pessimism that the national economy would continue to worsen and that the middle and working class participated less in the nation's prosperity compared to the upper class. In short, many voters were questioning whether the "American Dream" was still attainable and they were looking for a candidate that would revitalize their optimism.[36]

Regarding the primaries, the situation changed significantly in the days before Barack Obama's "Yes, we can" speech. The clear favourite Hillary Clinton was defeated by Barack Obama in the first election in Iowa. Thus, Barack Obama was favoured for the primary in New Hampshire, but narrowly lost it to Hillary Clinton.[37]

This defeat meant for Barack Obama that he needed to provide voters with a compelling reason to vote for him as the person who could start the change being needed to reinvigorate the "American Dream".[38]

---

[34] See Frank, H. (2008) p. 3f.
[35] See Gotoff, D. (2007) *The Changing U.S. Voter*, p. 17f.
[36] See Gotoff, D. (2007) p. 17ff.
[37] See Frank, H. (2008) p. 4.
[38] See Frank, H. (2008) p. 4f.

4.2   Main topics of the speech

The overarching themes of the speech were "Hope" and "Change". I will analyse more specifically Barack Obama's claim for change in politics, unifying the American nation, his political agenda,[39] as well as his references to the "American Dream". Where possible, I will also briefly discuss the key rhetorical devices used in the speech.[40]

4.2.1   Change in politics

As noted above, the focus of Barack Obama's campaign was "Hope" and "Change We Can Believe In"[41] and this included changing politics in order to make a better life – the "American Dream" – more achievable. For Barack Obama, this change in politics was already underway in the consciousness of the American people. Directly after the introduction of his speech, he gave the following examples[42] in which he addressed how different social groups took it upon themselves to bring change to the United States:

- "There is something happening when men and women in Des Moines and Davenport, in Lebanon and Concord, come out in the snows of January to wait in lines that stretch block after block because they believe in what this country can be."[43]
- "There's something happening when Americans who are young in age and in spirit, who've never participated in politics before, turn out in numbers we have never seen because they know in their hearts that this time must be different."[44]
- "There's something happening when people vote not just for party that they belong to, but the hopes that they hold in common."[45]

Barack Obama concluded his appeal for change in politics by emphasizing:[46]

> "That's what's happening in America right now; change is what's happening in America".[47]

Rhetorically, Barack Obama used a variety of repetition techniques in order to give more power to his statements and to make them more persuasive to the audience. One of them is the anaphora,[48] "There is something happening [...]", which he repeated at the start of every example to reinforce his demand for "Change".[49]

---

[39] See Frank, H. (2008) p. 7ff.
[40] For the rhetorical analysis of the speech only the written transcript will be used and not the TV recording.
[41] See Blake, A. *Obama: The man of many slogans*, p. 1.
[42] See Frank, H. (2008) p. 8.
[43] Transcript Speech, lines 16ff.
[44] Transcript Speech, lines 20ff.
[45] Transcript Speech, lines 24f.
[46] See Frank, H. (2008) p. 8.
[47] Transcript Speech, lines 29f.
[48] In rhetoric, anaphora is the repetition of the same word or a phrase at the beginning of sentences.
    See Zimmer, J. (2011) *"Rhetorical Devices: Anaphora." Manner of Speaking*, p. 1.
[49] See Frank, H. (2008) p. 8.

In many speeches Barack Obama favoured the rhetorical device of tricolon, also called the "Rule of Three" or the "Power of Three", i.e. the use of three words or three phrases to underline his messages.[50] An example mentioned above is "[...] men and women in Des Moines and Davenport, in Lebanon and Concord [...]".[51]

4.2.2 Unifying the American nation

At the time of the speech for Barack Obama, unifying the American nation was a major task. He accused the incumbent Bush administration of having separated the people and communities, making them distrust each other. Barack Obama wanted to unify the Americans across party lines as well as across all population groups[52] who were bound together by one goal, that was to achieve "Change":

- "And whether we are rich or poor, black or white, Latino or Asian, whether we hail from Iowa or New Hampshire, Nevada or South Carolina, we are ready to take this country in a fundamentally new direction."[53]
- "Democrats, independents and Republicans who are tired of the division and distraction that has clouded Washington [...]"[54]

Again, tricolons such as "Democrats, independents and Republicans" and "rich or poor, black or white, Latino or Asian" dominated his statements. The contrasts made in the tricolons which were used here reflect the different groups of society. The population of America consists of people with different social status, nationalities, ethnical backgrounds, education and political opinions, that often do not match; but nonetheless Barack Obama believed that the people can be united by one common target. From a rhetorical perspective, the use of opposites and contrasts make arguments stronger and make speeches more memorable.[55]

Barack Obama created the term "our new majority"[56] and added everybody to this group that shared his goals. The term "our new majority" was intended to connect all his followers and like-minded people. In the concluding section of his speech, he revisited this union of all Americans that "we are one nation"[57] addressing examples from different parts of the country and social classes:[58]

"And so, tomorrow, as we take the campaign south and west, as we learn that the struggles of the textile workers in Spartanburg are not so different

---

[50] See Leanne, S. (2009) p. 119.
[51] Transcript Speech, lines 16f.
[52] See Frank, H. (2008) p. 9.
[53] Transcript Speech, lines 26ff.
[54] Transcript Speech, lines 34f.
[55] See Edgar, D. (2013) p. 2ff.
[56] Transcript Speech, line 45.
[57] Transcript Speech, line 108.
[58] See Frank, H. (2008) p. 9.

than the plight of the dishwasher in Las Vegas, that the hopes of the little girl who goes to the crumbling school in Dillon are the same as the dreams of the boy who learns on the streets of L.A., we will remember that there is something happening in America, that we are not divided as our politics suggest, that we are one people, we are one nation".[59]

In this quote Barack Obama referred indirectly to the "American Dream" when he mentioned the hopes of the little girl and the dreams of the boy were equal.

4.2.3   Barack Obama's political agenda

Barack Obama's political agenda focused on making health care affordable to more people, realigning the tax burden, combatting the impact of climate change, improving education and strengthening foreign and security policies.[60]

The health care reform was Barack Obama's very top priority and lighthouse project. He believed that by providing affordable health care insurance to every American will enable everybody to achieve the "American Dream":

"Our new American majority can end the outrage of unaffordable, unavailable health care in our time."[61]

Barack Obama wanted a fairer tax policy. American people, especially the working and middle class, should get tax releases while the wealthy should contribute more and especially the corporations should be penalized if they destroy jobs in the United States. To convey a clear message that could be understood by everybody, he used a metaphor when he demanded to put the "tax cut in the pockets of working Americans who deserve it."[62] There was a direct link to the "American Dream" because if the working Americans had more money it would help them to achieve it:

"Our new majority can end the tax breaks for corporations that ship our jobs overseas and put a middle-class tax cut in the pockets of working Americans who deserve it."[63]

Another goal was to reform education. Barack Obama cited improved educational opportunity as a fundamental aspect of helping the next generation to achieve the "American Dream". This aspect was important to many of the voters as they feared the situation would worsen for their children due to the fact that they would not

---

[59] Transcript Speech, lines 102ff.
[60] The achievements of Barack Obama's political targets will be analyzed in chapter 5.2.
[61] Transcript Speech, lines 39ff.
[62] Transcript Speech, lines 46f.
[63] Transcript Speech, lines 45ff.

achieve upward mobility without a good education as a basis.[64] He sought to improve access to good education by enhancing the quality of education. This included the school infrastructure as well as the better recognition of teachers by increasing their income:

> "We can stop sending our children to schools with corridors of shame and start putting them on a pathway to success. We can stop talking about how great teachers are and start rewarding them for their greatness by giving them more pay and more support."[65]

For Barack Obama, fighting against effects of climate change and, specifically, the need to transition from fossil fuels to renewable green energy was a central topic:

> "[…] free this nation from the tyranny of oil and save our planet from a point of no return." [66]

In order to safeguard the "American Dream" Barack Obama wanted to improve the security of the United States. He also recognized the role that the military plays and sought to give both the active military as well as military veterans proper recognition and support:

> "We will end this war in Iraq. We will bring our troops home. We will finish the job -- we will finish the job against Al Qaida in Afghanistan. We will care for our veterans."[67]

Following his election manifesto, he listed the counterarguments of his political opponents. He did this without any direct criticism. However, by using the introduction "We have been […]"[68] he generalized the criticism of his opponents by referring the critics also to all his followers: [69]

- "We have been told we cannot do this by a chorus of cynics."[70]
- "We've been asked to pause for a reality check."[71]
- "We've been warned against offering the people of this nation false hope."[72]

Additional rhetorical elements used above are the frequent use of personal pronouns, in particular "we", to bridge the gap between him as a speaker and the audience. Barack Obama successfully utilized pronouns to win the hearts and minds of the audience and to personalize his messages.[73] Examples[74] are "We know […]", "We have been told […]" and "We've have been asked […]".

---

[64] See Gotoff, D. (2007) p. 19.
[65] Transcript Speech, lines 48ff.
[66] Transcript Speech, lines 54f.
[67] Transcript Speech, lines 58ff.
[68] Transcript Speech, line 80.
[69] See Frank, H. (2008) p. 10.
[70] Transcript Speech, line 80.
[71] Transcript Speech, line 82.
[72] Transcript Speech, lines 82f.
[73] See Leanne, S. (2009) p. 74ff.
[74] Transcript Speech, lines 74ff.

In many of the examples described in this chapter Barack Obama used descriptive words like "corridors of shame", "pathway to success", "tyranny of oil", to illustrate pictures making his political messages for better education and green energy more memorable.[75]

4.2.4 References to the "American Dream"

The climax of the speech was when Barack Obama wanted to motivate the people who had felt disenfranchised to believe in the "American Dream" again. He hoped to motivate them to believe that they could overcome challenges such as global terrorism, climate change, education, health care and tax reform and by doing so achieving the greater social as well as economic opportunity and equality characterized by the "American Dream". The slogan "Yes, we can" was intended to convey that for the Americans everything is possible with will and optimism.[76]

With the reference to the "single creed"[77] and its main principles being freedom, equality, justice and humanity, Barack Obama wanted to express his belief that the American people together could live up to the "American Dream":[78]

> "[...] generations of Americans have responded with a single creed that sums up the spirit of a people: Yes, we can. Yes, we can. Yes, we can."[79]

Barack Obama referred to occurrences of major importance in American history that seemed to be unreachable. The way he integrated these historic events into his speech made it easier for the listener to understand the context. Below, there are several historical occurrences that he named in his speech.[80]

Barack Obama referred to the Declaration of Independence and the Bill of Rights when he mentioned the founding documents of the United States of America that helped to guarantee the "American Dream":

> "It was a creed written into the founding documents that declared the destiny of a nation: Yes, we can."[81]

He highlighted the concept of equality of people, when he pointed out that slaves and abolitionists strived to have freedom:

> "It was whispered by slaves and abolitionists as they blazed a trail towards freedom through the darkest of nights: Yes, we can."[82]

---

[75] See Leanne, S. (2009) p. 85f.
[76] See Frank, H. (2008) p. 10f.
[77] Transcript Speech, line 87.
[78] For the explanation of "American Creed" see also chapter 3: The "American Dream".
[79] Transcript Speech, lines 86-88.
[80] See Frank, H. (2008) p. 10f.
[81] Transcript Speech, lines 89f.
[82] Transcript Speech, lines 91f.

He named the dream of the immigrants and pioneers to have a better life:

> "It was sung by immigrants as they struck out from distant shores and pioneers who pushed westward against an unforgiving wilderness: Yes, we can."[83]

Finally, Barack Obama referred to one of the most important aspects for the "American Dream" which is opportunity and prosperity. He promised to restore the "American Dream" and even to make the world a better place for all:

> "Yes, we can, to opportunity and prosperity. Yes, we can heal this nation. Yes, we can repair this world. Yes, we can."[84]

From a rhetorical view, the examples above show again the use and effectiveness of an anaphora, in particular the continuously used slogan "Yes, we can". This slogan was used as a catchphrase to focus the audience's attention.[85]
In addition, the above-mentioned examples contained many alliterations, which added more power to his words to encourage his supporters to remain inspired.[86]
The following are examples of alliterations used as an emphasis to the messages that Barack Obama sought to deliver:

- "[...] documents that declared the destiny [...]"[87]
- "[...] trail towards freedom through the darkest of nights [...]"[88]
- "[...] pioneers who pushed westwards [...]"[89]

In this last part of his speech, Barack Obama appealed to the emotions of the people. As can be seen from the historical examples, "Hope" was always the key element to achieve positive changes. His intention was to use these examples in order to motivate his listeners to believe in the "American Dream" again.

Many American presidents used the "American Dream" to motivate the people but Barack Obama in particular proved to have the rhetorical competence to reach the hearts of his compatriots by using "those appropriate words from the American political lexicon, drawing on [...] shared, cherished socio-political values."[90]

The constant repetition of the slogan "Yes, we can" in this context suggested to the listeners that the "American Dream" could continue and that his above-mentioned goals such as change in politics, unifying the American nation and Barack Obama's political agenda could be achieved together by the American people.

---

[83] Transcript Speech, lines 93ff.
[84] Transcript Speech, lines 100f.
[85] See Leanne, S. (2009) p. 185.
[86] See Leanne, S. (2009) p. 115f.
[87] Transcript Speech, lines 89f.
[88] Transcript Speech, lines 91f.
[89] Transcript Speech, lines 93f.
[90] Leanne, S. (2009) p. 54f.

5   Evaluation of Barack Obama's political agenda

The last chapter will work out if Hillary Clinton's accusation "all rhetoric, no substance" was correct and how Barack Obama fulfilled the political promises of his "Yes, we can" speech.

5.1   Hillary Clinton's statement "all rhetoric, no substance"

During the primary campaign, the tone and the personal confrontation between Barack Obama and Hillary Clinton was very harsh, especially on the part of Hillary Clinton. One of her plans was to weaken Barack Obama's central messages of "Hope" and "Change". Her own strategy was to position herself as a realist who understands the necessary qualities of a president. She repeatedly accused Barack Obama and his supporters of being naive and innocent.[91]
For months during the campaign, Hillary Clinton blamed Barack Obama of being "all rhetoric, no substance".[92] She also complained: "It's time we moved from good words to good works, from sound bites to sound solutions [...]"[93]
The overall assumption behind this criticism was that Barack Obama tended until then to deliver a good speech but no substance.[94]
Hillary Clinton's accusation of "all rhetoric, no substance" is a frequent reproach in politics as well as in everyday life. It is an accusation often used to criticize some-one who only makes promises that will not be kept and backed by actions.[95]

Even if the campaign was very competitive between both candidates, Barack Obama later appointed Hillary Clinton secretary of state, and both worked together in a surprisingly good partnership.[96]

5.2   Achievement of Barack Obama's political agenda

In order to analyse if Hillary Clinton's above-mentioned accusations were correct the achievements of Barack Obama's political agenda in respect to his "Yes, we can" speech will be analysed based on various media articles. As there is some bias in media of the United States, the facts are sometimes difficult to be assessed. Moreover, there are often no clear statistics that give a clear comparison of the situation before and after Barack Obama´s presidency.

---

[91] See Bosman, J. (2008) *Clinton turns from anger to sarcasm*, p. 1f.
[92] Hayes, S. F. (2008) *Obama and the Power of Words*, p. 2.
[93] Hayes, S. F. (2008) p. 2.
[94] See Hayes, S. F. (2008) p. 3.
[95] See Writing explained. *What Does All Talk No Action Mean?* p1ff.
[96] See Landler, M., Cooper, H. (2010) *After a Bitter Campaign, Forging an Alliance*, p. 1ff.

The health care reform, "Obamacare", was one of most the important political goals. Before "Obamacare", a general government-run health plan for all Americans didn't exist[97] and people were at risk for financial ruin if they needed an expensive medical treatment. The estimated cost of "Obamacare", which passed Congress in 2010 was US$ 940 billion.[98] The following numbers show that "Obamacare" was a success because from 2008 to 2016 the number of Americans without health insurance dropped by 15.2 million to 28.6 million, which means that in 2016 only 9% of all Americans still did not have health insurance. However, as a critical side note, costs of health cover continued to rise faster than wages or general inflation.[99]

The evaluation of his tax reform showed that Barack Obama made several tax cuts both for private citizens and corporations in order to stimulate the economy after the financial crisis. Overall his tax policy helped to get the United States out of the problems caused by the financial and economic crisis of 2008.[100]

Lacking meaningful statistics that refer to the exact time of Barack Obama's presidency, the success of his educational reform is difficult to measure and to assess. The only objective proxies to validate the outcome are the changes in expenditure for educational institutions and the number of 16-to 24-year olds, who were neither enrolled in school nor working. From 2008 to 2015, the expenditure for educational institutions changed from US$ 1,089 billion (7.4% of the GDP[101]) to US$ 1,254 billion (7.0% of the GDP) in 2015.[102] Even if the total amount of expenditure increased, the percentage in respect of GDP was reduced. This can only be evaluated as partly successful.

The number and percentage of people in the 16 to 24 year old age group who were neither enrolled in school nor working in 2006, in respect of the above-mentioned age group, was 4,569,000 or 12.4%, out of a total of 36,822,000.[103] In 2016, the number of people in this age group was 38,480,000, and 5,059,000 were neither enrolled in school nor working, i.e. the percentage of these increased to 13.1%.[104] In this respect, Barack Obama did not fulfil his promise.

[97] Aside from Medicare for the elderly and Medicaid for the very poor. See HHS (2019) p. 1.
[98] See Rodrigues, J. (2017) *The Obama years: timeline of a presidency*, p. 3.
[99] See Brooks, J. (2017) *Obama's Final Numbers*, p. 17ff.
[100] See Amadeo, K. (2019) *Obama Tax Cuts Facts and Consequences*, p. 1f.
[101] GDP = Gross Domestic Product which is the total market value of the goods and services produced by a country's economy. See Bondarenko, P. (2019). *Gross domestic product*, p. 1.
[102] See Snyder, T. D. (2018, February) *N. C. Statistics*, Ed., Table 106.10, p. 63.
[103] See Snyder, T. D. (2018, February) Table 501.30, p. 680.
[104] See Snyder, T. D. (2018, February) Table 501.30, p. 682.

With regard to the salary and support of the teachers, the statistics show that the median earnings of teachers in the 25- to 29-year old age group with a bachelor's degree in education (all kinds of educational institutions) in 2015, went up from US$ 38,260 in 2010 to US$ 38,960, i.e. an increase of 1.8%. Thus, an improvement was achieved during Barack Obama's presidency; but compared to the development of the median earnings of all bachelor degrees which increased by 3.0%,[105] it was below average.

Even though some referred to Barack Obama as America´s first climate president, he only concentrated on the climate topic in the final stage of his presidency, however, with considerable success. On a national level, he banned new oil and gas drilling in most United States owned waters in the Atlantic and the Artic. On an international level, he made clear that the world was facing no threat greater than climate change and he was one of the drivers to reach the Paris Agreement[106] in 2016.[107]

Finally, Barack Obama's achievements for the United States foreign policy, security and military are assessed. In May 2011, Osama bin Laden, leader of Al Qaida, was killed by United States Navy SEALs in Pakistan, which was a big success in the fight against international terrorism. Seven months later, Barack Obama formally declared the end of the Iraq war.[108] He pulled American troops out of Iraq in 2011, but began sending troops back in 2014, after the Islamic State fighters occupied large parts of the country.[109] Veteran care was overall a success, as the number of homeless individual veterans dropped from more than 74,000 in 2010 to 40,000 in 2016.[110] Overall, it looks like Barack Obama kept his promises but was forced to reconsider his troop drawback due to the difficult situation in Iraq.

To sum it up, it can be said that Barack Obama had very ambitious political targets to meet his promises to revitalize the "American Dream" for the Americans. The above analysis shows a mixed result in terms of how he accomplished his initial political agenda. Reasons for this are partly that after 2010 the Democrats lost control of Congress and that Barack Obama had severe opposition from the Republicans.[111] Barack Obama's greatest achievement was the implementation of the health care reform - one of the central themes in his New Hampshire speech.

---

[105] See Snyder, T. D. (2018) Table 505.10, p. 710.
[106] The Paris Agreement's central aim is to fight the threat of climate change by keeping a global temperature rise this century below 2 degrees. See United Nations. (2018). *The Paris Agreement*, p. 1ff.
[107] See Milman, O. S., & others (2017) p. 2f.
[108] See Rodrigues, J. (2017) *The Obama years: timeline of a presidency*, p. 5.
[109] See Brooks, J. (2017) *Obama's Final Numbers (factcheck.org, Ed.)*, p. 26.
[110] See Shane III, L. (2017) *Number of homeless vets rises for first time in seven years*, p. 1.
[111] See Zelizer, J. (2018) *Obama's legacy: He sparked hope – and got blindsided*, p.1ff.

6   Conclusion

It is highly probable that Barack Obama's life, his New Hampshire "Yes, we can" speech, becoming the first African American president and his view on the "American Dream" will get a special place in history books. In many ways, his life story is the "American Dream" and this formed the basis of his "Yes, we can" message. With his hopeful visions for "Hope" and "Change" and his efforts to achieve that vision, Barack Obama made his way to the hearts of many people, and will not only be remembered in America, but also worldwide.

Barack Obama successfully used the concept of the "American Dream" to deliver the key messages in his "Yes, we can" speech. Like many former presidents of the United States he utilized the "American Dream" in a political speech to motivate the nation. In the difficult situation that the United States faced at that time of the speech, Barack Obama reminded his compatriots that with his demands to change politics, to unify the Americans and his political agenda, the "American Dream" is within reach of everyone.

As a result of his appealing political agenda and his rhetorical skills to deliver his messages, many Americans started to believe in him. The "Yes, we can" speech, brought him back into the race for nomination to become the Democratic candidate for president of the United States of America.

Hillary Clinton accused Barack Obama during the Democratic nomination process to be "all rhetoric, no substance".[112] It is widely accepted that Barack Obama is one of the most talented speakers in America's history and that he knows how to use rhetorical skills to inspire and motivate people. In hindsight the allegation was part of Hillary Clinton's nomination campaign. Later she supported Barack Obama during his presidency as secretary of state.

Barack Obama was clearly a visionary already during the 2008 nomination process and during his presidency. The analysis[113] of his political goals shows a mixed picture of accomplishment, but Barack Obama clearly achieved his top priority "Obamacare".

Overall, the campaign slogan "Yes, we can" and the messages for "Hope" and "Change We Can Believe In' in the New Hampshire primary speech summarize Barack Obama's vision for a better life - the "American Dream".

---

[112] Hayes, S. F. (2008) p. 2.
[113] See chapter 5.2.

Bibliography

BOOKS

Cullen, Jim. *The American Dream: A Short History of an Idea That Shaped a Nation*. Oxford New York: University Press Paperback, 2004.

Frank, Harald. *Rhetorische Analyse der "Yes we can" Rede von Barack Obama*. Norderstedt: Grin Verlag GmBH, 2008.

Leanne, Shel. *Say It Like Obama - The Power Of Speaking With Purpose And Vision*. New York, Chicago, San Francisco, Lisbon, London, Madrid, Mexico City, Milan, San Dehli, San Juan, Seoul, Singapore, Sydney, Toronto: McGraw-Hill, 2009.

Obama, Barack. *Dreams from My Father*. New York: Broadway Paperbacks, 2004.

Obama, Barack. *The Audacity of Hope*. 2008: Canongate Books, n.d.

Truslow, Adams James. *THE EPIC OF AMERICA*. Boston: Little, Brown and Company, 1931.

Wilson, Kevin D. *The American Dream: In the Age of diminished expectations*. Washington, D.C.: Georgetown University, 2013.

ARTICLES, INTERNET

Amadeo, Kimberly. *Obama Tax Cuts Facts and Consequences*. Edited by the balance. 6th July 2019. https://www.thebalance.com/obama-tax-cuts-3306330 (accessed July 24th, 2019).

Black, Curtis. *The Birthplace of Community Organizing*. Edited by ChicagoStories.org. 16th July 2019.

Blake, Aaron. *Obama: The man of many slogans*. Edited by The Washington Post. 10th July 2012. https://www.washingtonpost.com/blogs/the-fix/post/president-obama-a-man-of-many-slogans/2012/07/10/gJQAf8UIaW_blog.html?noredirect=on&utm_term=.5d7accd57482 (accessed July 31st, 2019).

Bondarenko, Peter. *Gross domestic product*. Edited by Enceclopdia Britannica. 2019. https://www.britannica.com/topic/gross-domestic-product (accessed July 22nd, 2019).

Bosman, Julie. *Clinton turns from anger to sarcasm*. February 24th, 2008. https://thecaucus.blogs.nytimes.com/2008/02/24/clinton-turns-from-anger-to-sarcasm/ (accessed July 20th, 2019).

Britannica Encyclopedia. *Primary election*. Edited by Encyclopaedia Britannica. n.d. https://www.britannica.com/topic/primary-election (accessed July 16th, 2019).

Brooks, Jackson. *Obama's Final Numbers.* Edited by factcheck.org. 29th
September 2017. https://www.factcheck.org/2017/09/obamas-final-
numbers/ (accessed June 28th, 2019).

Courtright Patton, Marguerite. *The American's Creed.* 28th May 2010.
http://arkansas-dar.org/majorgraycreed.html (accessed October 7th,
2019).

Edgar, David. *'Yes we can' - Barack Obama's lesson in American rhetoric.* The
Guardian. 4th November 2013.
https://www.theguardian.com/books/2013/nov/04/barack-obama-lesson-
american-rhetoric (accessed July 29th, 2019).

Gotoff, Daniel. *The Changing U.S. Voter.* Edited by usinfo.state.gov. 2007.
http://usinfo.state.gov/journals/itdhr/1007/ijde/gotoff.htm (accessed April
20th, 2019).

Hayes, Stephen F. *Obama and the Power of Words.* The Wall Street Journal,
Feburary 2008.

HHS.Gov. *What is the difference between Medicare and Medicaid?* 2019.
https://www.hhs.gov/answers/medicare-and-medicaid/what-is-the-
difference-between-medicare-medicaid/index.html (accessed October
15th, 2019).

King Jr., Martin L. *American Rhetoric.* 28th August 1963.
https://www.americanrhetoric.com/speeches/mlkihaveadream.htm
(accessed July 27th, 2019).

Landler, Mark, and Helene Cooper. *After a Bitter Campaign, Forging and
Alliance.* The New York Times. 18th March 2010.
https://www.nytimes.com/2010/03/19/us/politics/19policy.html (accessed
October 7th, 2019).

Milman, Oliver/Ackerman, Spencer/Pilkington, Ed/Beckett, Lois/Rushe,
Dominic/Redden, Molly/Lartey, Jamiles/Borger, Julian/Glenza, Jessica,
and Milman, Oliver/Ackerman, etc. *Obama's legacy: the promises,
shortcomings and fights to come.* The Guardian. 3rd January 2017.
https://www.theguardian.com/us-news/2017/jan/03/barack-obama-
president-legacy-policy-issues-wins-fights (accessed June 27th, 2019).

Murse, Tom. *Why the New Hampshire Primary Is so Important.* 27th December
2018. https://www.thoughtco.com/why-the-new-hampshire-primary-is-
important-336752 (accessed June 16th, 2019).

National Archives. *Declaration of Independence: A Transcription.* Edited by
National Archives. n.d. https://www.archives.gov/founding-
docs/declaration-transcript (accessed July 27th, 2019).

Page, William Tyler. *The American's Creed.* UShistory.org. 1917.
http://www.ushistory.org/documents/creed.htm (accessed October 7th,
2019).

Rodrigues, Jason. *The Obama years: timeline of a presidency.* 3rd January 2017.
https://www.theguardian.com/us-news/2017/jan/03/the-obama-years-
timeline-of-a-presidency (accessed June 28th, 2019).

Shane III, Leo. *Number of homeless vets rises for first time in seven years.* 6th
December 2017.
https://www.militarytimes.com/veterans/2017/12/06/number-of-homeless-

veterans-nationwide-rises-for-first-time-in-seven-years/ (accessed June
28th, 2019).

Snyder, Thomas D./Dillow, Sally A. *Digest of Education Statistics 2016*.
www.nces.ed.gov. February 2018.
https://nces.ed.gov/pubs2017/2017094.pdf (accessed June 28th, 2019).

Transcript Speech. *Barack Obama's New Hampshire Primary Speech*.
https://www.nytimes.com/2008/01/08/us/politics/08text-obama.html.

United Nations. *The Paris Agreement*. Edited by United Nations. 22nd October
2018. https://unfccc.int/process-and-meetings/the-paris-agreement/the-
paris-agreement (accessed July 18th, 2019).

Wallenfeldt, Jeff, and David Mendell. *Barack Obama President of the United
States*. 19th June 2019. https://www.britannica.com/biography/Barack-
Obama (accessed July 14th, 2019).

Writing explained. *What Does All Talk No Action Mean?*
https://writingexplained.org/idiom-dictionary/all-talk-no-action (accessed
October 19th, 2019).

Zelizer, Julian. *CNN Opinion Obama's legacy: He sparked hope - and got
blindsided*. 11th March 2018.
https://edition.cnn.com/2018/03/09/opinions/obama-historian-legacy-
roundup-opinion-zelizer/index.html (accessed October 8th, 2019).

Zimmer, John. *Rhetorical Devices: Anaphora. Manner of Speaking*. 4th June
2011. https://mannerofspeaking.org/2011/06/04/rhetorical-devices-
anaphora/ (accessed July 10th, 2019).